AFRICAN AMERICAN
GRAHAM FAMILY
OF WAYNE COUNTY MISSISSIPPI
By James E. Graham Jr.

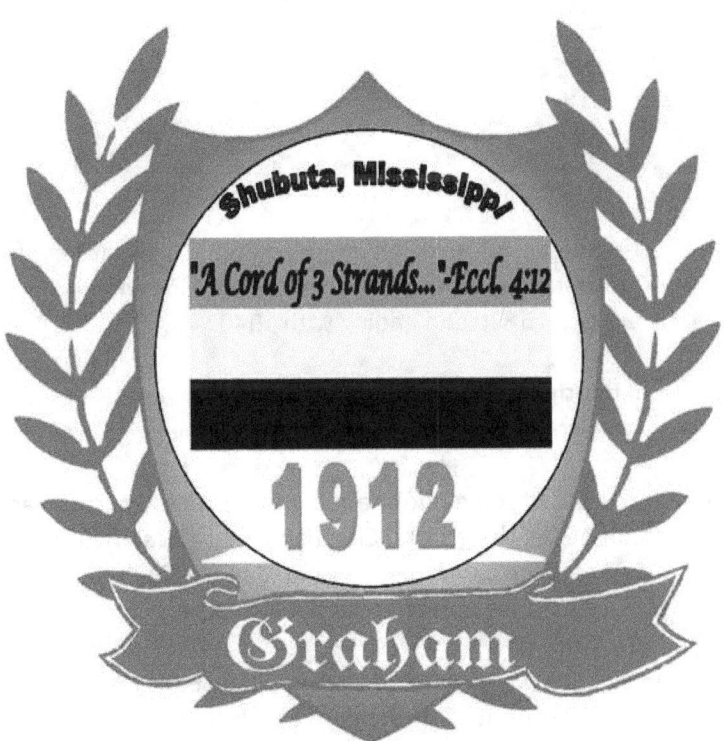

Photos and information have been gathered from various sources.
Scriptures used is from the Holy Bible.

The writer has based some information, primarily conversation and
statements on the general Christian culture of some in
the African American community. Included in The Graham Family
history are some hypothetical situations.

This publication was published by CreateSpace May of 2015.
The ISBN is located on the back of this publication.

To order additional copies of this publication go to www.amazon.com

Or write to:
James E. Graham Jr.
Post Office Box 653,
Napanoch New York 12458

TABLE OF CONTENT

The History of the African American Graham Family of Wayne County Mississippi

Before The 1870 Census

Our story begins in one of the Dark Ages of human history. The 1600's gave way to a massive wave of European hunters looking for black field hands on the west coast of Africa. Many of these American slaves came from the Mende People. Today this area is known as Sierra Leone. 1804, in American, our story continues with a West African slave girl giving birth to a baby girl named Morah. Years later, Morah and others would move from North Carolina to South Carolina, with slave-owner Peter Graham and his Scottish family.

What got Morah and her family through these dark times was stories like the royal Ethiopian who was baptized by the evangelist Philip. It is said that this Ethiopian would be responsible for spreading the good news about Jesus Christ to thousands across the continent of Africa. In South Carolina, Morah would give birth to a son. She called his name Peter. Peter would work as a farmer in South Carolina until the age of 27. From South Carolina to Mississippi, Morah along with Peter and others would move with slave-owner, Peter Graham and his Scottish family. Morah's family would be divided. Morah and her son Peter would be separated once in Mississippi. This would break Morah's heart.

Years had passed and Peter never thought it could really happen, black men free in America. At age 45, Peter and his wife Maneron had heard the good news. In the year 1863, President Abraham Lincoln signed the Emancipation Proclamation, setting black slaves free. Maneron would shout, "Hallelujah to The Lamb of God! Thank you Jesus, we're free!"Peter would call a family meeting that night, things were changing. At the meeting were his wife Maneron, His daughter Mona, and his two young sons George and Lonzo "Loringus".

The Census of 1870: 1st and 2nd Generations

Seven years later from the Emancipation, not much had changed; most whites still saw and savagely treated blacks less than human. But there was the census that recorded the status of all Americans, regardless of their skin color. In 1870, Peter and his family along with other black families living on the farm in Wayne County of Mississippi, would line up for the country wide census. Peter was 50, his wife Maneron was 60, his daughter Mona was 17, his son George was 13, and his youngest son Lonzo was 9.

The Census of 1880: 1st and 2nd Generations

10 years later, the 1880 census had come, and many things for Peter had changed. The good, he had reunited with his son named R.R. The bad, Maneron, his wife had passed away. Life was moving, his oldest children, Mona, George and Lonzo "Loringus" all had moved out. His mother Morah and others had moved in, coming from the other side of Mississippi to Wayne County. Morah loved being close to Peter and his family. Morah would be the one to remind the family of their West African roots, she would sometimes refer to herself as "Morah the Mende". What a difference 10 years made. Peter and his family along with other black families living on the farm in Wayne County Mississippi, would line up for the country wide census. Peter was 60, his mother Morah was 76, his daughter Loren from North Carolina was 18, and R.R. was 14.

The Census of 1900: 3rd Generation

In the 1900 census, Peter is said to have returned to South Carolina. His son Lonzo "Loringus" Graham would continue the Graham legacy in Wayne County Mississippi. The Census records Lonzo "Loringus" being married to Eliza Graham with their 5 children. At the time of the census Lonzo "Loringus" is 38, his wife Eliza is 32, his sons Allen is 12, Oscar 7. His daughter Ora is 14, Mary 11, and Caldonia 9 years of age.

The Census of 1910, 1920, 1930 & 1940: 4th Generation

In The 1910 census, Lonzo "Loringus" oldest son Allen continues the Graham Legacy. Allen and his wife Mollie are both 22. His sister Ora is 25 and Caledonia 19. His younger brother Oscar was 17 years old. In the 1920 census, Allen and Mollie are both age 32 with 4 children. Their daughter Thelma is 9. They have 3 sons, Laranzie 8, Lucheour" Lushus" 7, and Fred 5 years old.

In the 1930 census, Allen and Mollie are 42, Thelma is now 19, Lushus is 17 and Fred is 15. Laranzie at 18 had moved out.

In 1940, Thelma and Lushus "Lucius" moved out and Allen and Mollie were both 50 years old with 3 more children. 25 year old Fred is still at home, he helps out with Hattie Mae age 5; Charley 3 and Wille F. age 1.

Year 1940: 5th and 6th Generations

At this time, 1940, Lushus "Lucius" and Pinkie have 3 children. Their names are Marvin (6), Jesse James (4), and Robert (2). Lushus is 28 and Pinkie (Pope) of Shubuta Mississippi is 25. Pinkie being a child of Rev. Marzean and Nancy Pope makes sure to pass her faith and love for The Holy Bible down to her children. This was the time of the "Great Migration" when many black families from Mississippi and other southern states moved to the North for better opportunities and less racism. Lushus "Lucius" and Pinkie would move their family to Albany New York. They would have 3 more children. Their names are Mary Nancy, Ed, and Percy Lee.

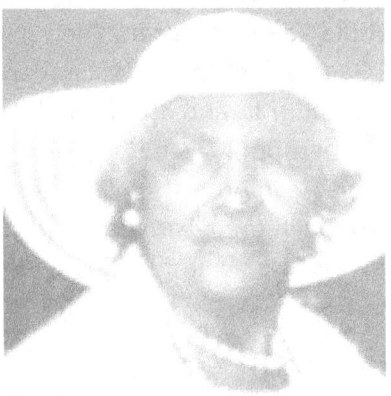

Year 1950-1970: 7th Generation

Between the 1950's and 1970's Rev. Marvin L. Graham Sr. would have 11 children. Marvin L. Graham Jr., James E. Graham Sr., Laverne Graham, Renee Graham, Janice Graham, Gayle Graham, Marvina Graham, David Graham, Arletta Graham, Rachel Graham and Elizabeth Graham. His brother Robert Graham would have 4 children. Their names are Eddie Graham, Alicia Graham, Reginald Graham, and Laura Graham. Ed "Bubba" Graham would have 5 children. Their names are Frank Graham, Brandon Graham, Melanie Graham, Tiffany Graham and Sha Graham. His sister, Mary Nancy would have 4 children. Their names are Shana, Stacy, Scott, and Nell.

Year 1970-1980: 8th Generation

Between 1970's and 1980's Marvin L. Graham Jr. would have 3 children. Their names are Marvin L. Graham III, Curtis Graham and Nathan Graham. James E. Graham Sr. and Mearies (McCarthy) Graham would have 8 children. Their names are James E. Graham Jr., Danta Graham, Jevell Graham, Tameka Graham, Tiffany Graham, Kamel Graham Tashay Graham and Tashemia Graham. Laverne would have 6 children. Their names are LaJuan McQueen, Archie McQueen Jr., Julius McQueen, Latoya McQueen, Joseph McQueen and Juan McQueen. Janice would have 2 children. Their names are Donelle and Danielle. Gayle would have 4 children. Their names are Wille, Dawana, Tashana, and Juaneika.

The 2000's: 8th and 9th Generations

David Graham Sr. would have 2 children. Their names are David Jr. and Amelia. The 8th Generation: Marvin L. Graham III, LaJuan McQueen, James E. Graham Jr. and other family members would give birth to the 9th Generation. Over 150 years have passed since the Emancipation of blacks in American, 9 Generations later, The Graham Family still thrive in their Christian Faith, Family and Fellowship with each another. Morah Graham would have been proud of her family.

THE 5TH GENERATION OF THE GRAHAM FAMILY

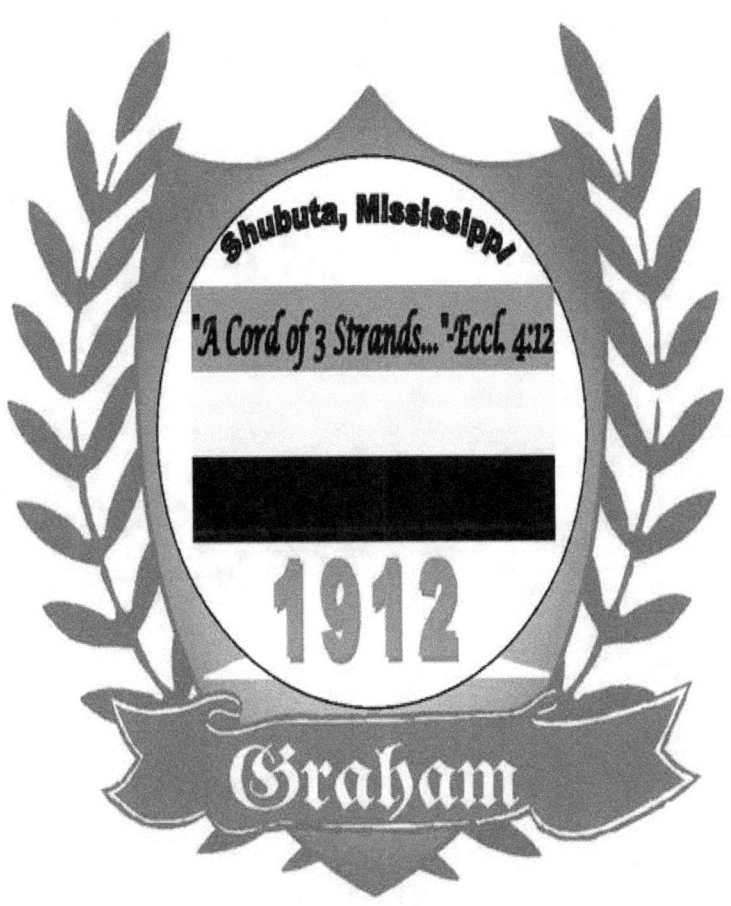

PINKIE (POPE) GRAHAM
BORN: 1915

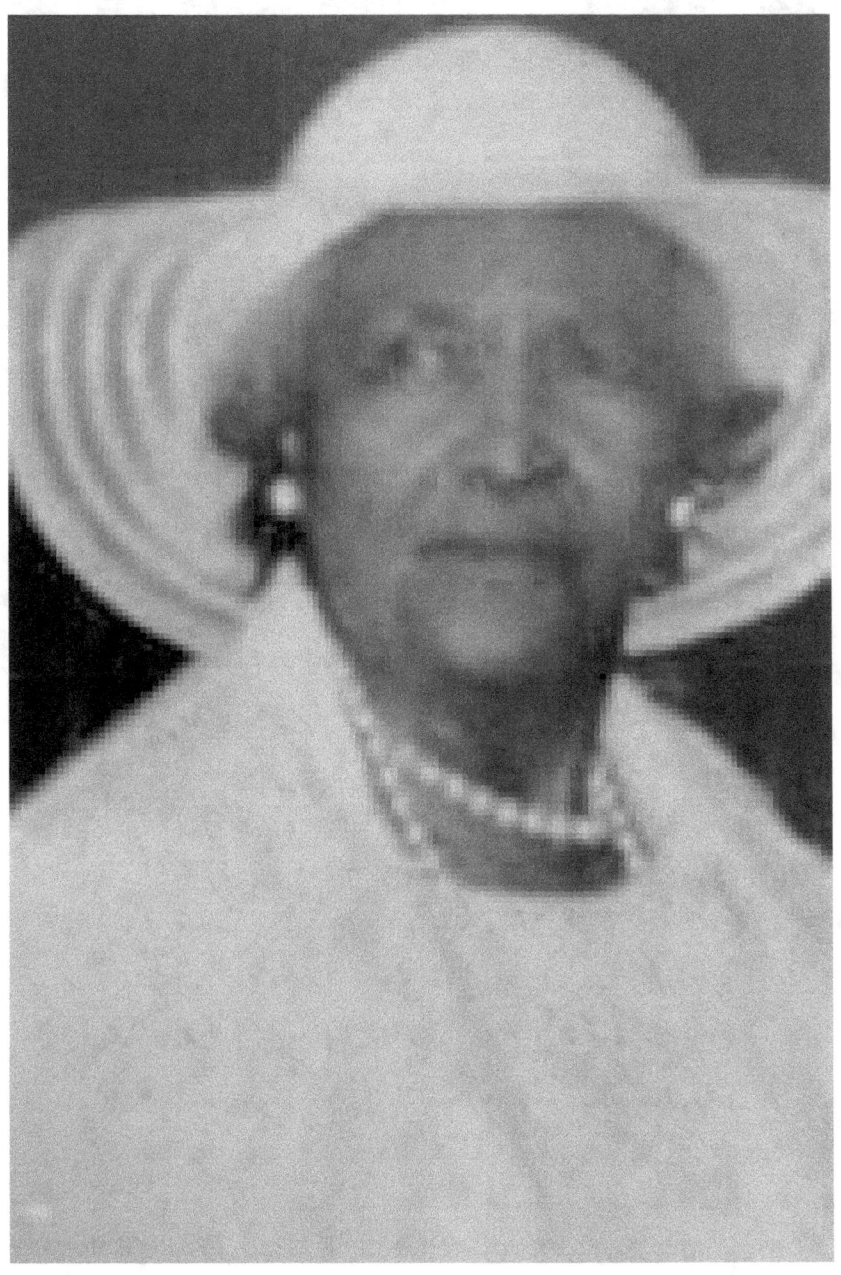

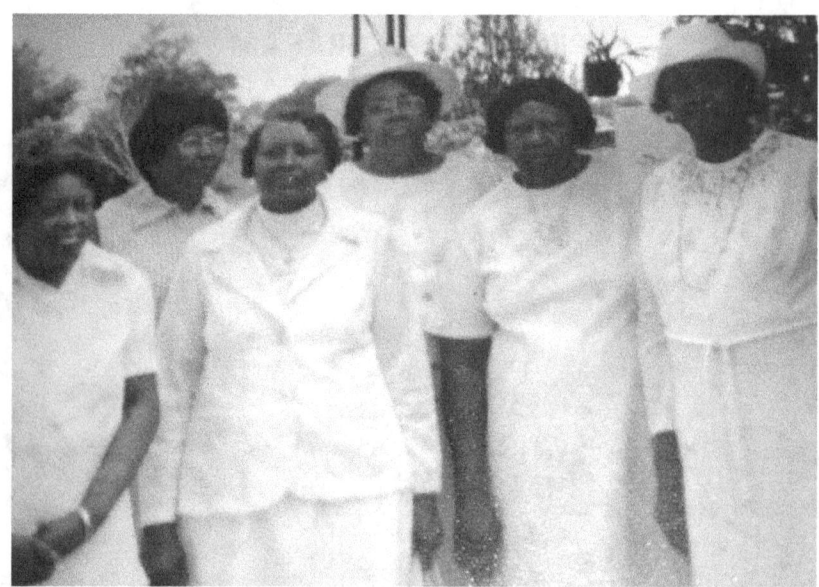

Pinkie (Pope) Graham pictured with her sisters: Zella, Wille Mae, Laura Trotter, Detha, and Mamie.

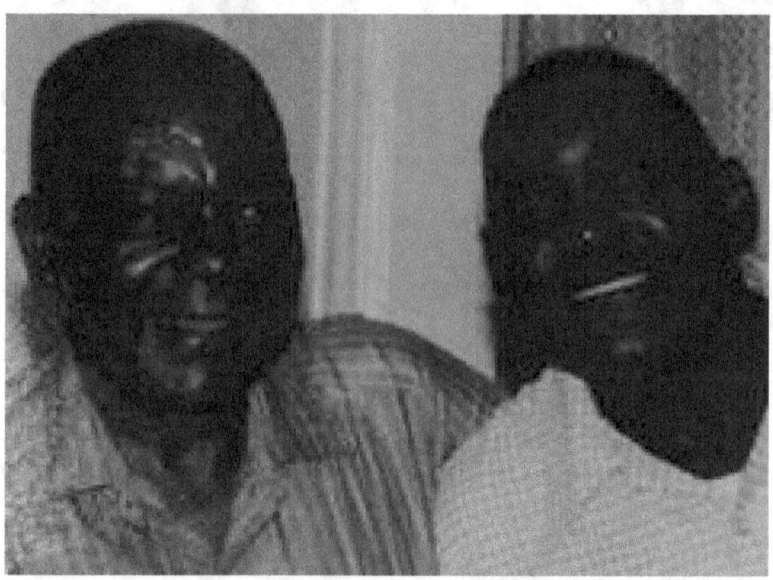

Lucius "Lushus" Graham pictured with his brother Fred Graham.

THE 6TH GENERATION OF GRAHAM FAMILY

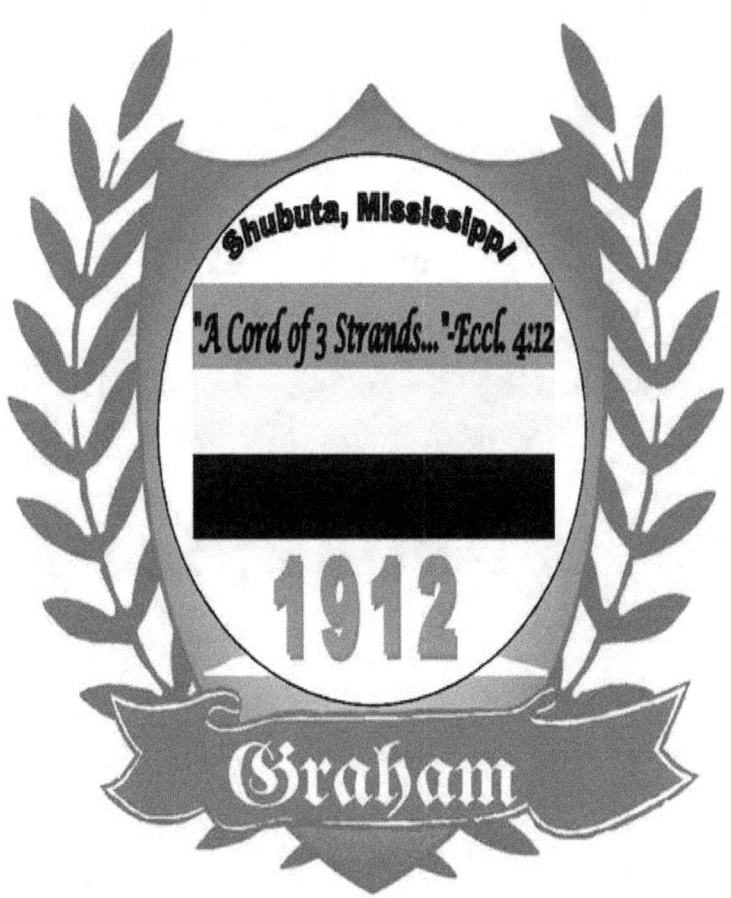

ED "BUBBA"GRAHAM

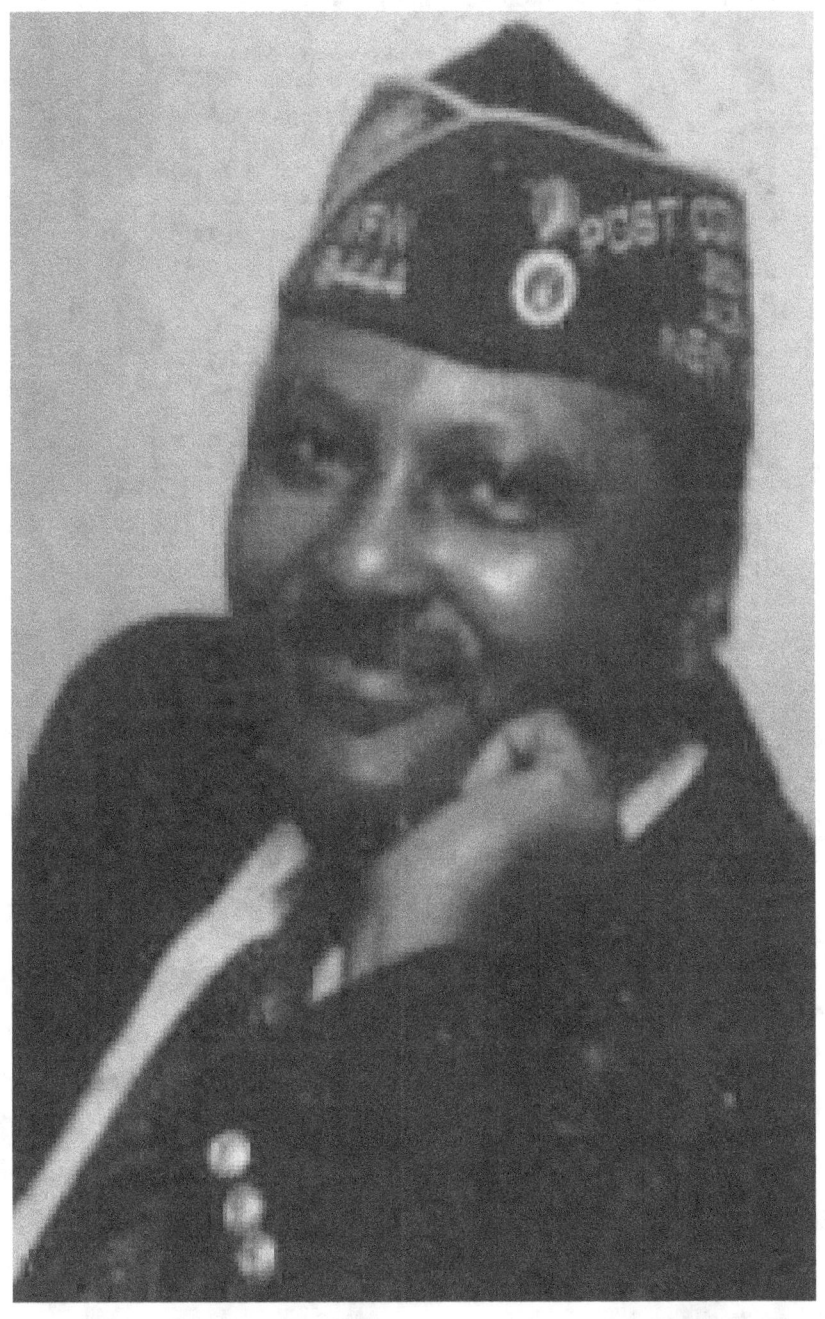

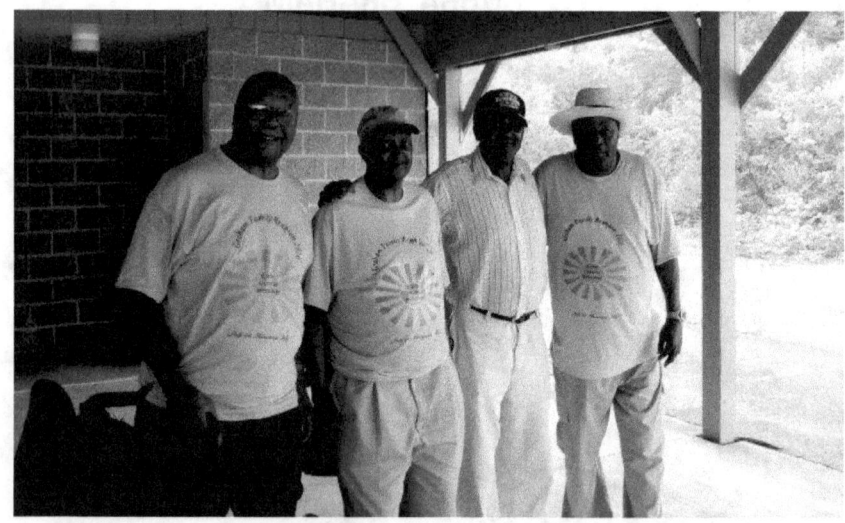

Rev. Marvin L. Graham Sr. pictured with his brothers: Jesse James Graham, Ed "Bubba" Graham and Percy Lee Graham.

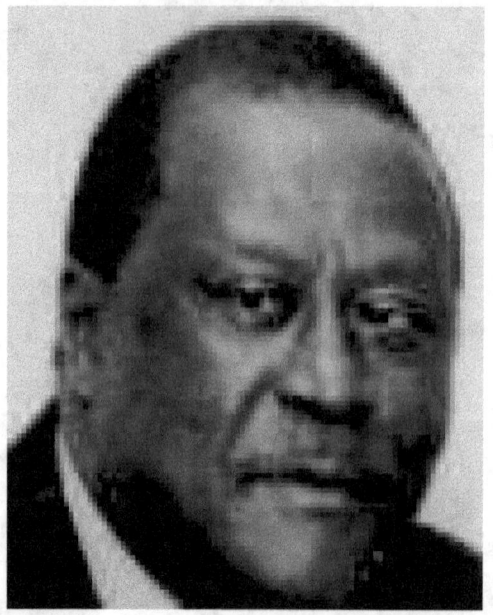

Percy Lee Graham.

THE 7TH GENERATION OF THE GRAHAM FAMILY

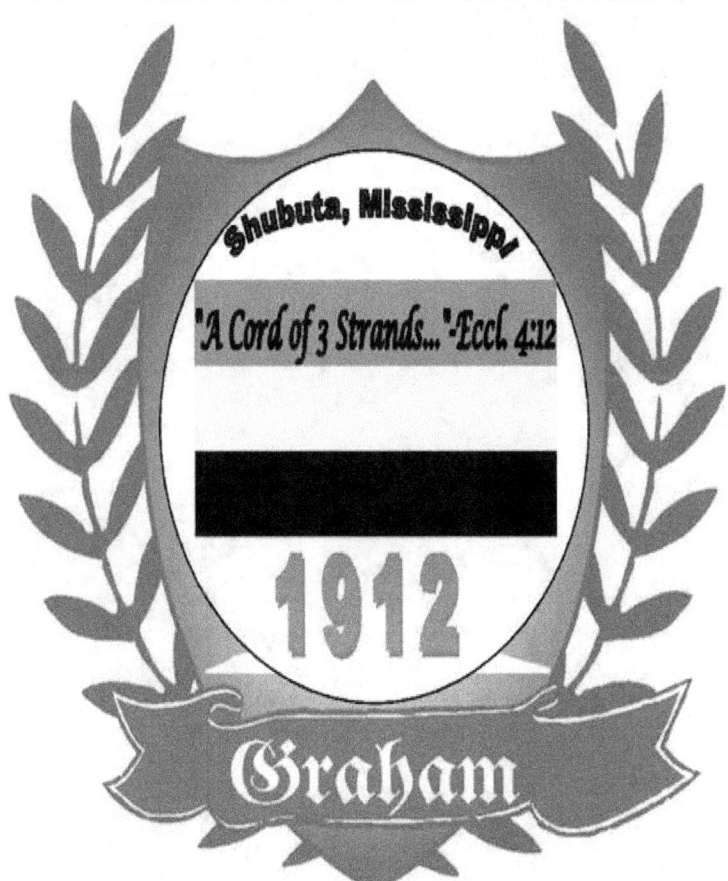

MARVIN L. GRAHAM JR.
JAMES E. GRAHAM SR.
LAVERNE (GRAHAM) MCQUEEN
WITH MOM: LILLIAN (NELSON) EDMUNDS

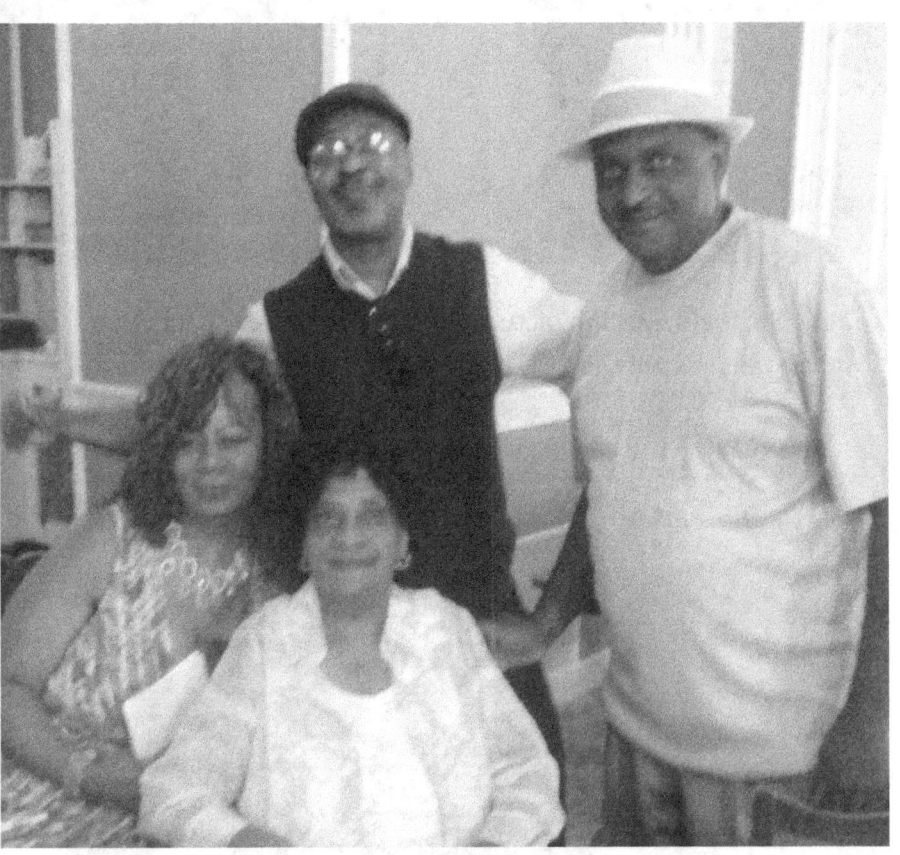

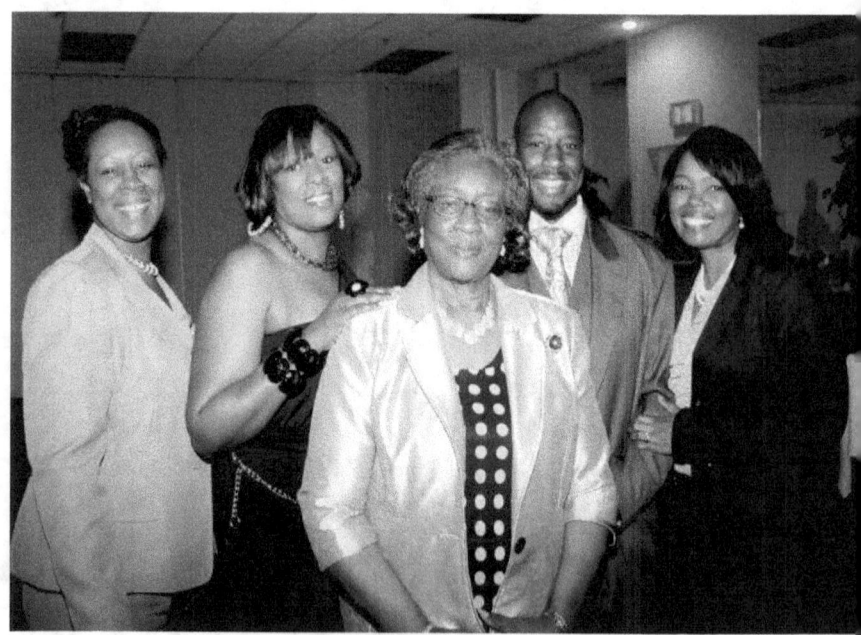

Rev. Reginald Graham pictured with mom Helen, sisters Laura and Alicia, and his wife.

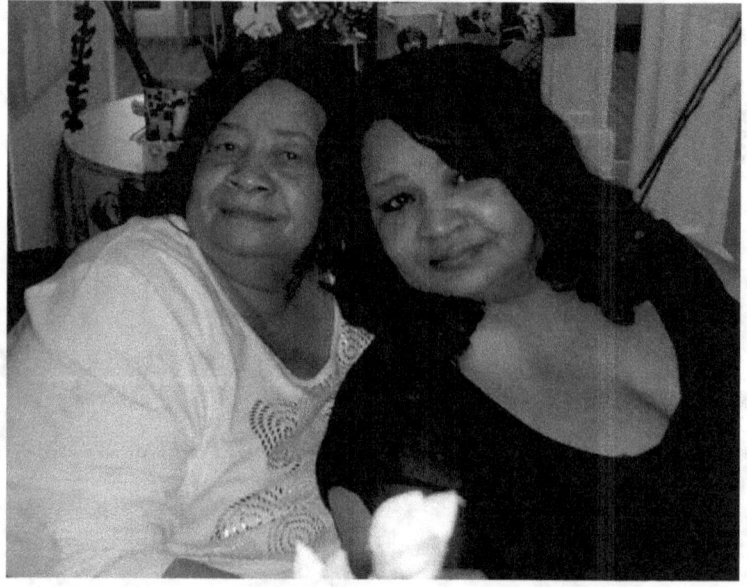

Gayle Graham pictured with her mom Ida Mae.

BRANDON GRAHAM WITH
STACEY ARRINGTON

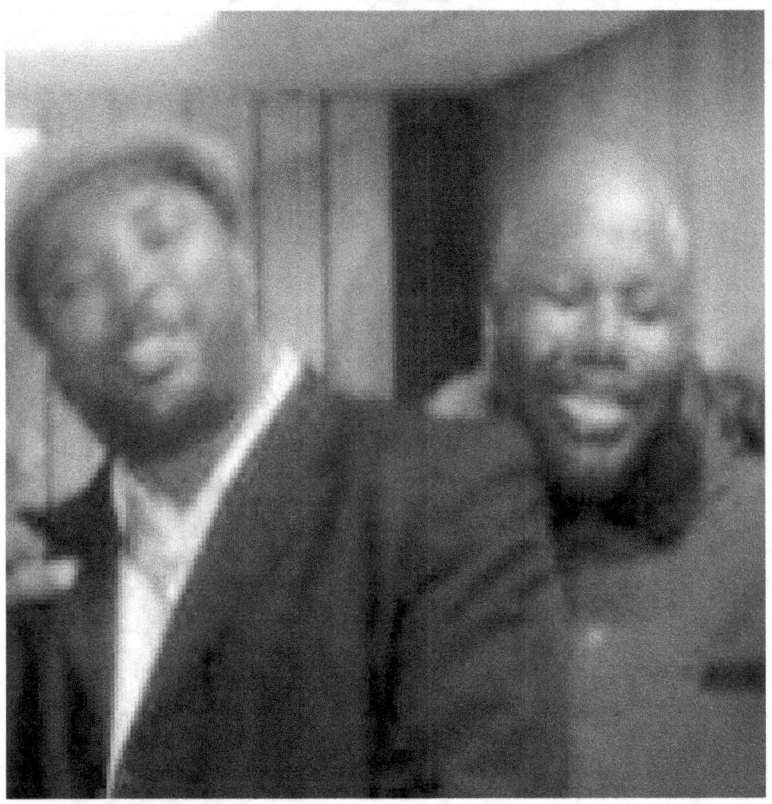

First cousins: Brandon Graham, son of Ed "Bubba" Graham and Stacey Arrington, son of Mary Nancy (Graham).

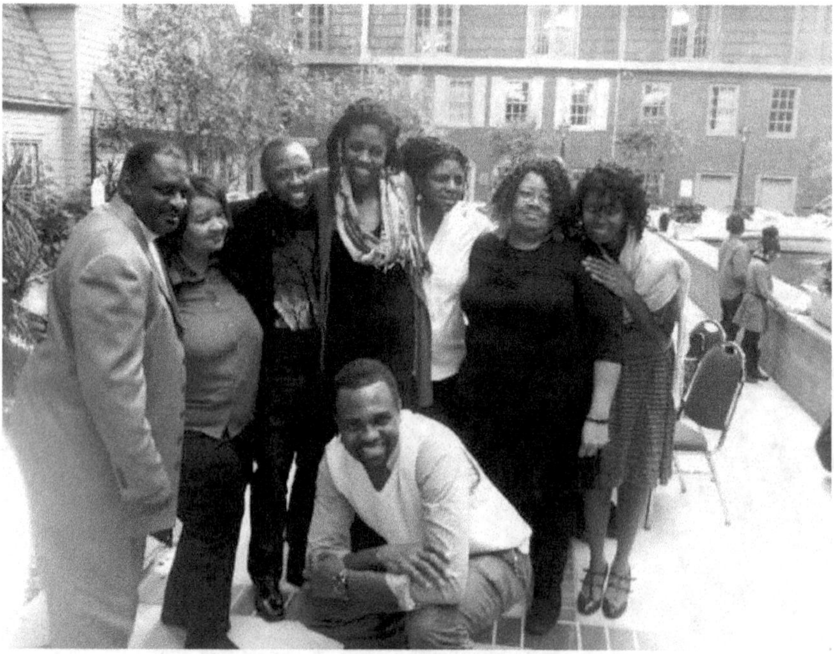

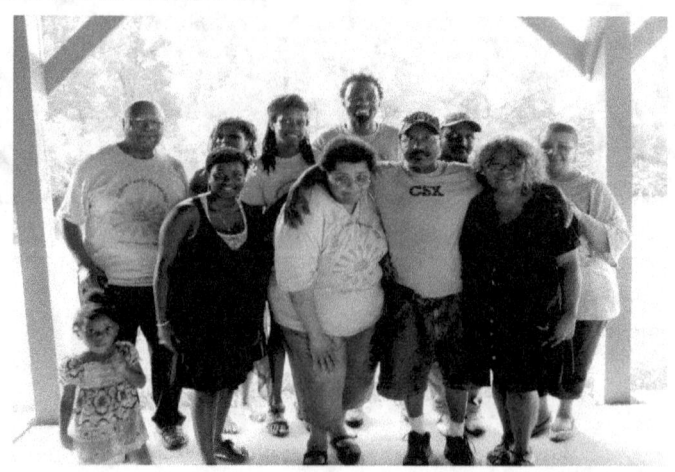

James E. Graham Sr. pictured with Gayle Graham, Arletta Graham, Elizabeth Graham, Marvina Graham, Janice Graham, Rachel Graham and David Graham Sr.

Rev. Marvin L. Graham Sr. pictured with his Children.

THE 8TH GENERATION OF GRAHAM FAMILY

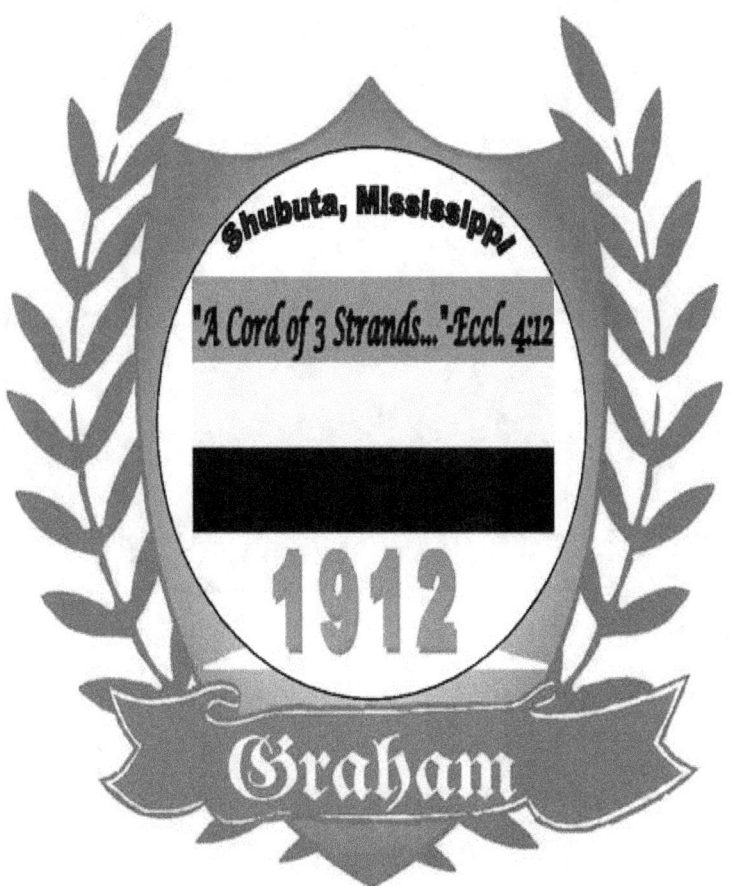

JAMES E. GRAHAM JR.
LAJUAN MCQUEEN
MARVIN L. GRAHAM III

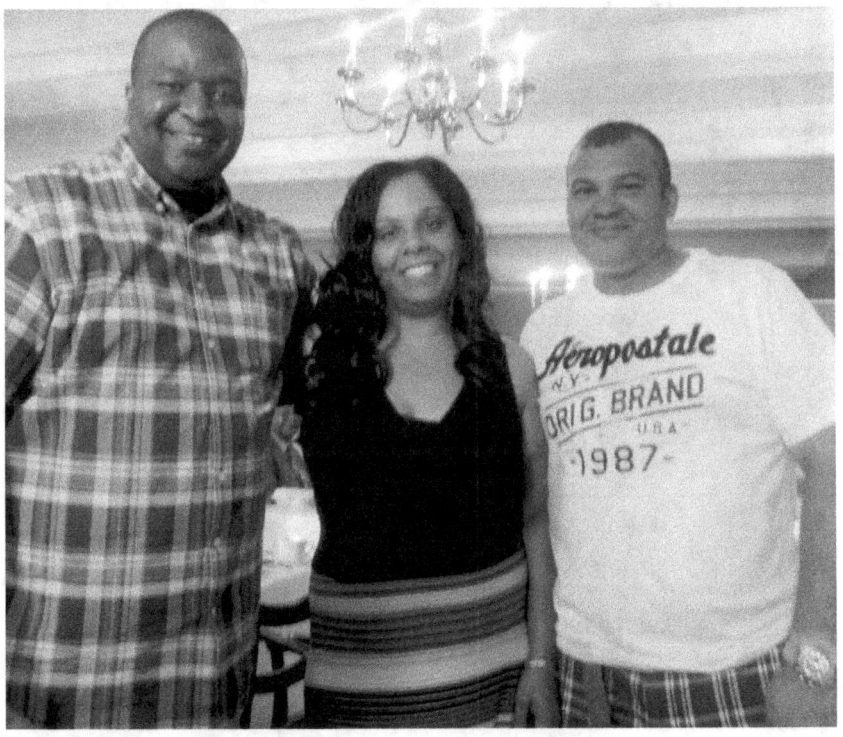

First cousins: James E. Graham Jr. son of James E. Graham Sr.,
LaJuan McQueen daughter of Laverne (Graham) McQueen and
Marvin L. Graham III son of Marvin L. Graham Jr.

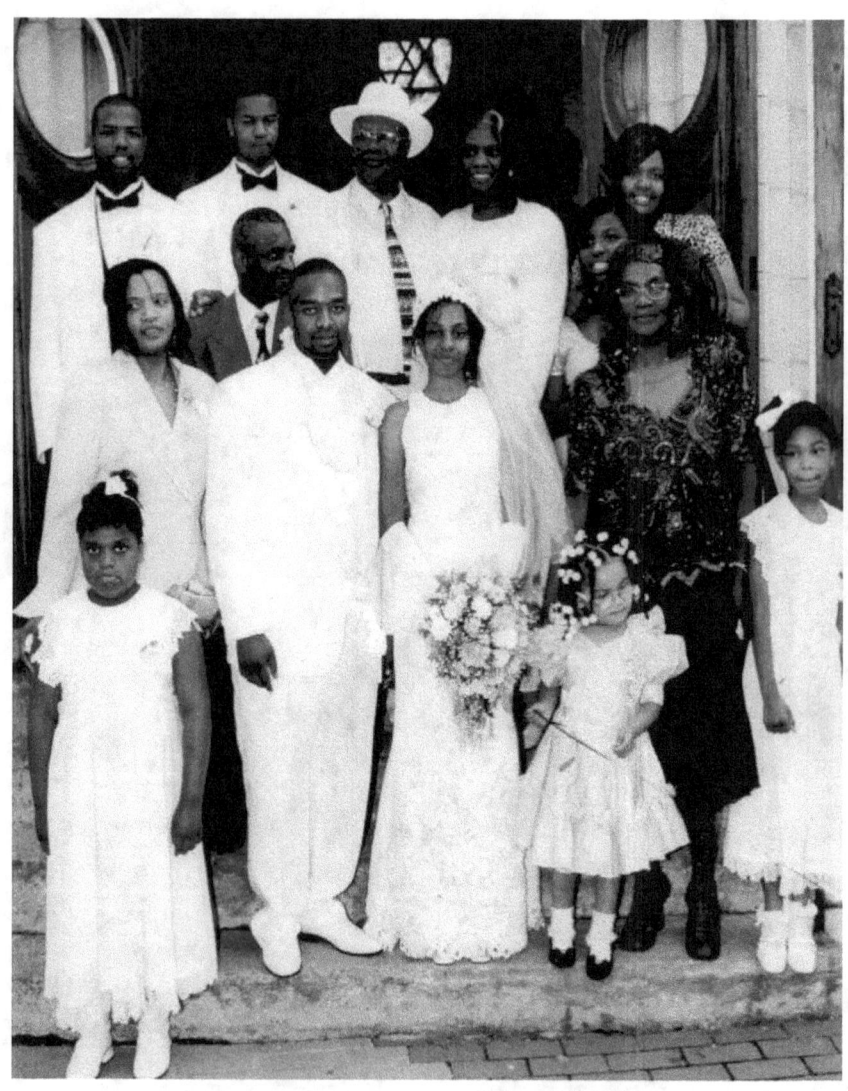

Rev. Marvin L. Graham Sr. and wife Diane Graham pictured with James E. Graham Sr. and wife Mearies (McCarthy) Graham, The bride and groom: James E. Graham Jr. and wife Kirsten L. (Speller) Graham. Jevell Graham, Danta Graham, Tameka Graham, Tiffany Graham, Tashay Graham, Tashemia Graham, Betty Grace (McGill) McCarthy and Jade McCarthy.

MULTI-GENERATIONAL PHOTOS

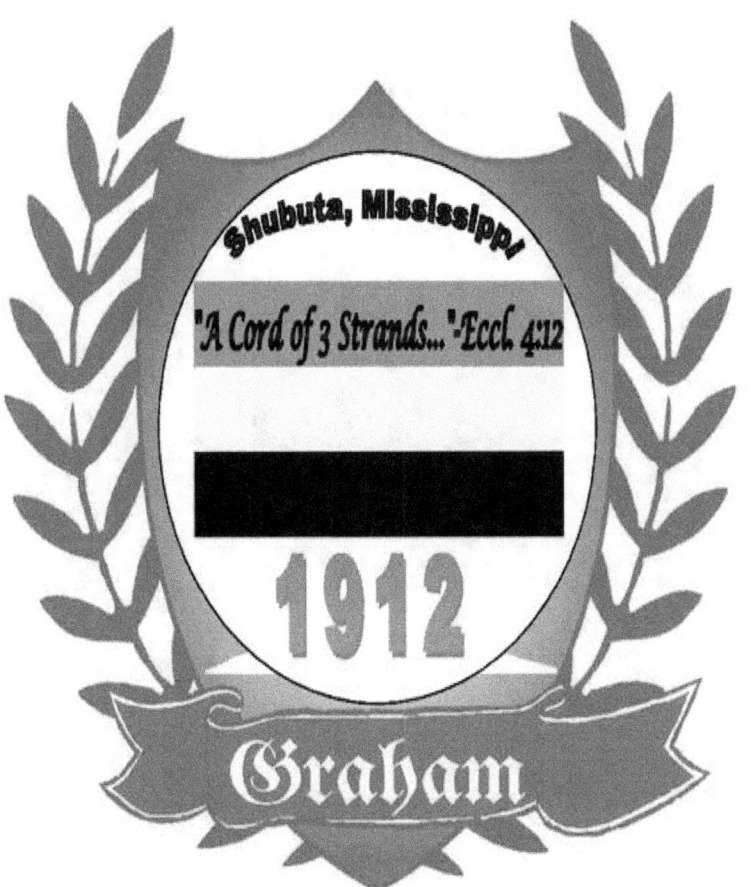

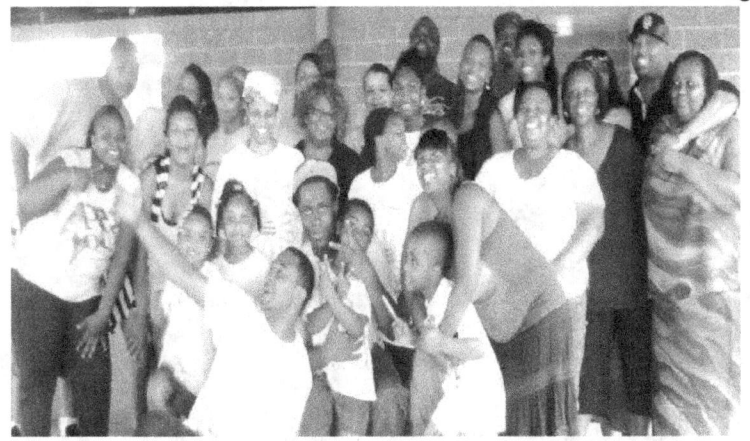

Family Reunion: 2010

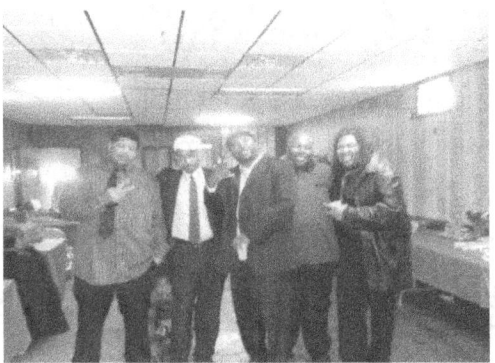

Graham men pictured at The Percy Lee Graham Repast.

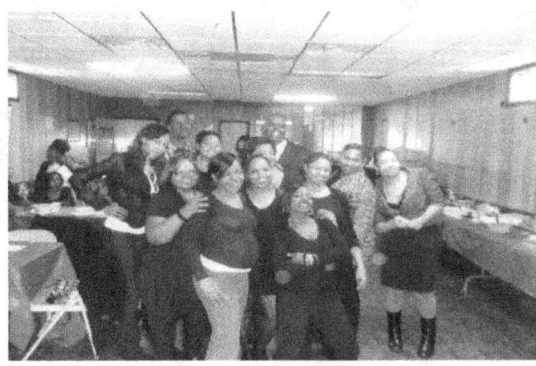

Graham women pictured at The Percy Lee Graham Repast.

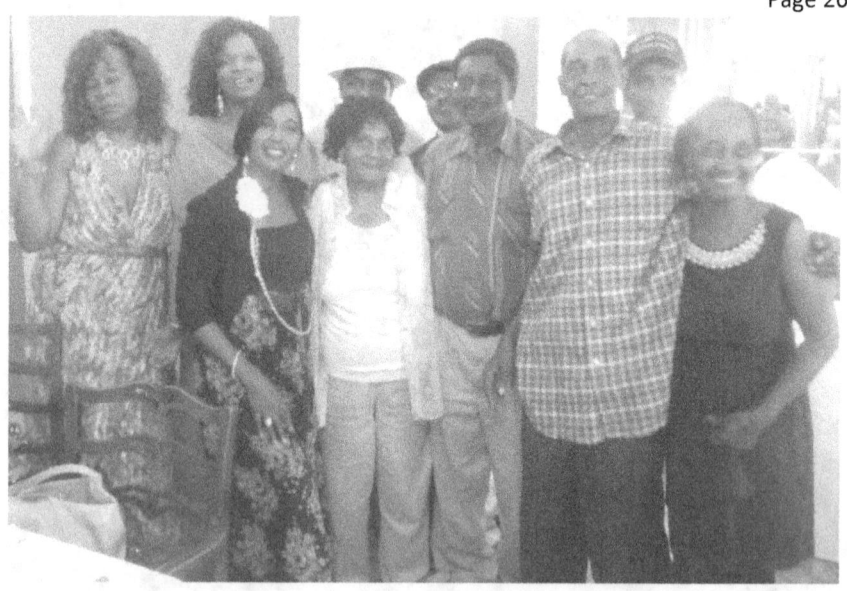

Lillian (Nelson) Edmunds pictured with Margaret, Robert, Seymour, Mary-Helen "Sister" McFarland and family.

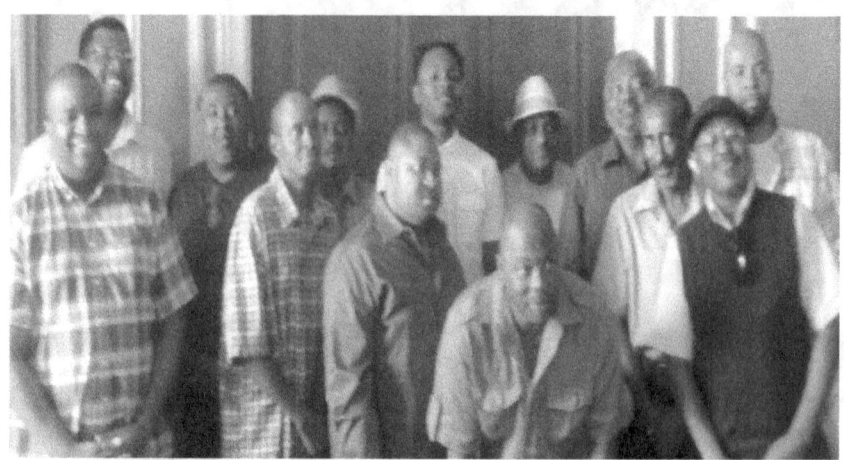

Marvin L. Graham Jr. pictured with Leroy Nelson, the Mcfarlands, James E. Graham Jr., Jevell Graham, Albert Nelson, Robert McFarland and kin, James E. Graham Sr., Luther Nelson, and Archie McQueen Jr.

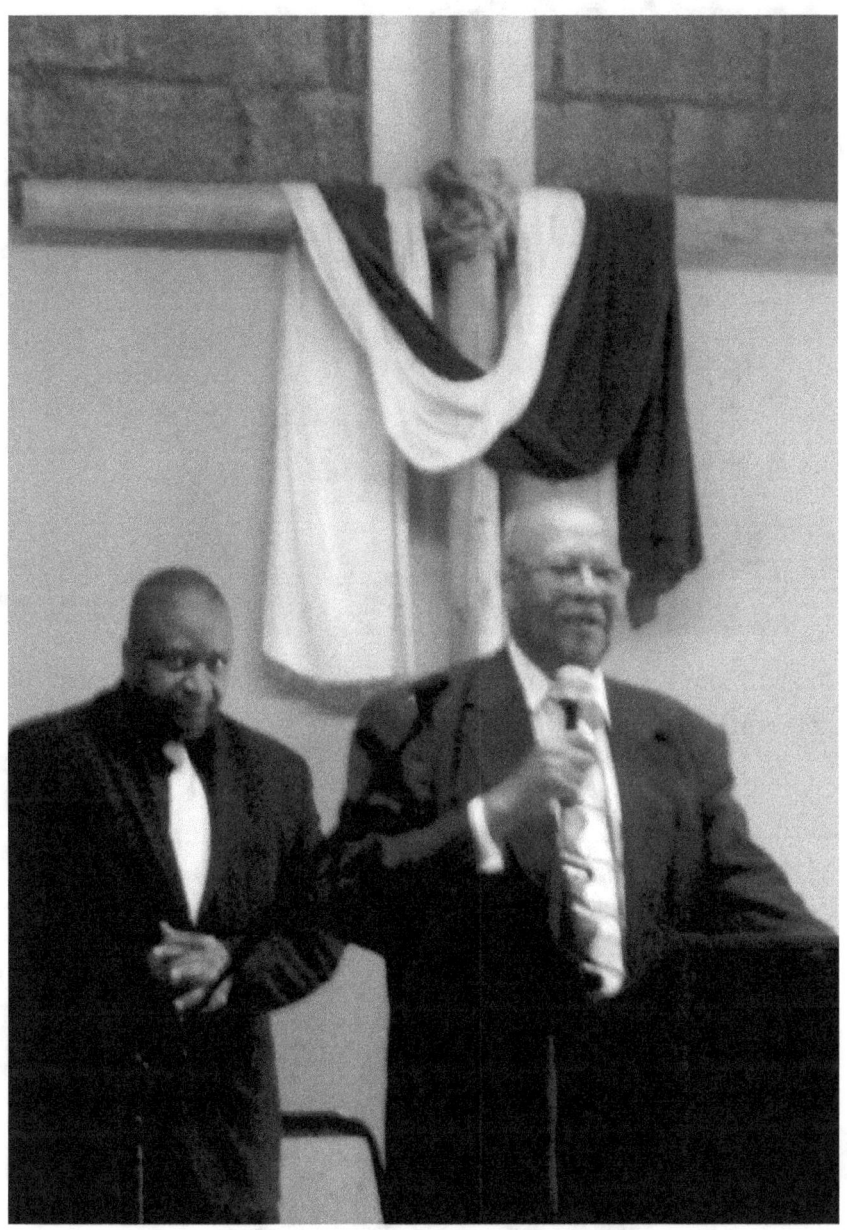

Rev. Marvin L. Graham Sr. pictured with grandson Rev. James E. Graham Jr.

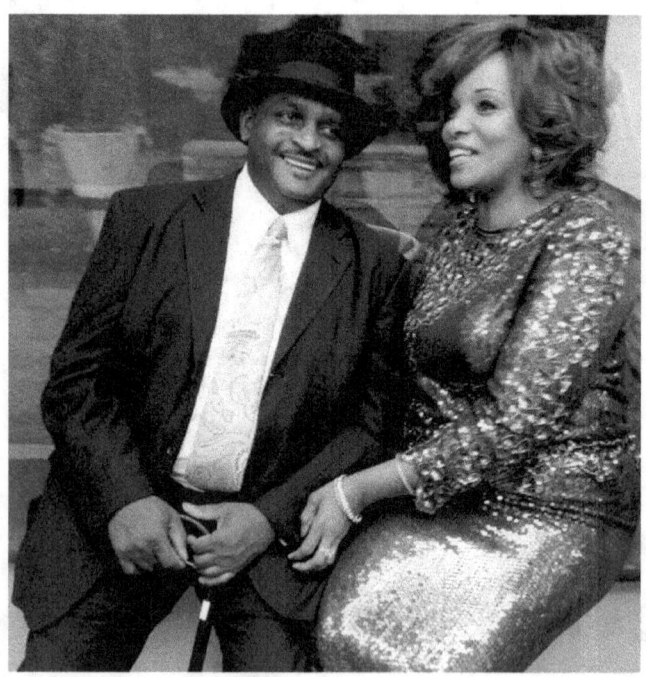

In 2015 James E. Graham Sr. and Mearies (McCarthy) Graham celebrate 40 years of Marriage.

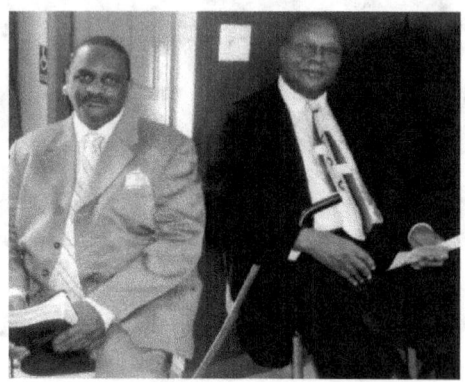

Deacon James E. Graham Sr. pictured with
Rev. Marvin L. Graham Sr. at Church service.

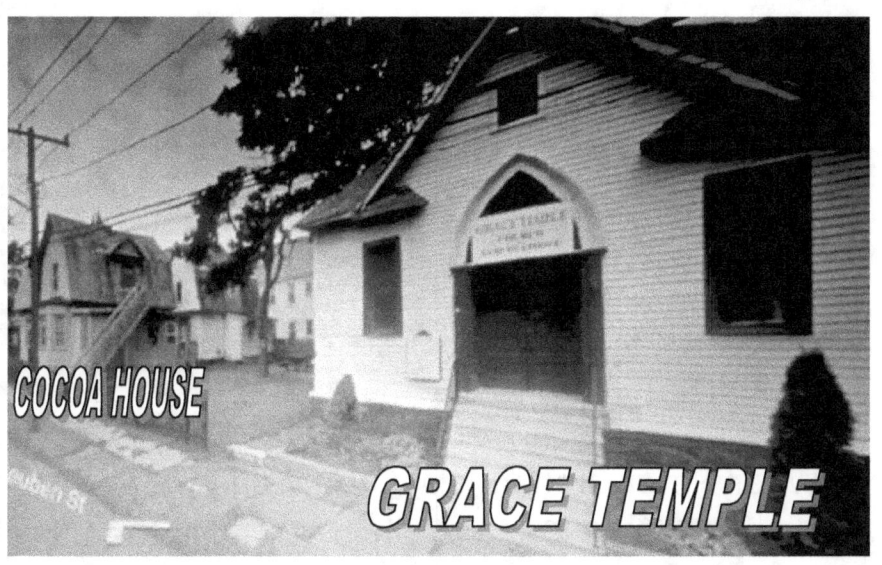

"A GREAT GRAHAM LEGECY!"

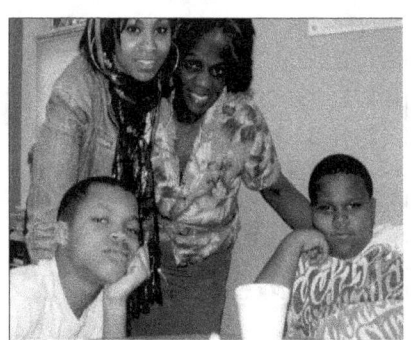
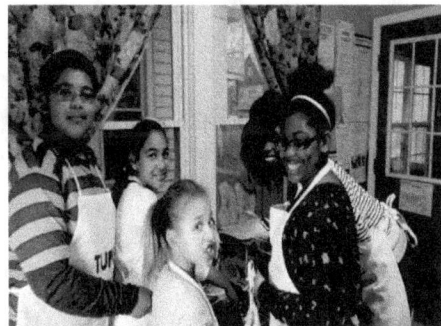

Latoya McQueen with Lady Diane Graham at the Cocoa house.
Founder of Cocoa house Rachel Graham with community children.

C.O.C.O.A: Children of Our Community Open to Achievement.

HELPING OTHERS HAS ALWAYS BEEN A STAPLE FOR THE GRAHAM
FAMILY. WE SEE PASTOR MARVIN L. GRAHAM SR. AND LADY
GRAHAM MINISTERING AT GRACE TEMPLE COGIC. WE ALSO SAW
THEIR DAUGHTER, RACHEL GRAHAM; CREATE THE COCOA HOUSE
WHICH HAS MENTORED TO MANY COMMMUNITY CHILDREN, IN
ADDITION TO FEEDING AND EDUCATIONAL PROGRAMS.

DID YOU KNOW?	
When Morah Graham was 59 in 1863...	President Abraham Lincoln signed The Emancipation Proclamation.
When Peter Graham was 56 in 1876...	14 African Americans had served in the US Congress between 1870-1876.
When Allen Graham was 22 in 1910...	The Famous African American Scholar, W.E.B. Dubois organized the NAACP.
When Lushus "Lucius" Graham was 17 in 1929...	The Famous African American civil rights leader and Christian preacher Dr. Martin Luther King was born.

A QUICK LOOK AT OUR JOURNEY!

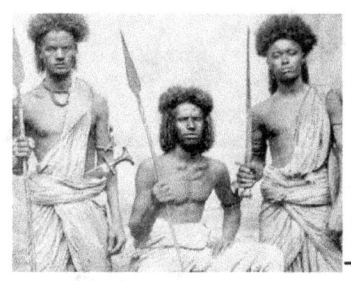-1600-1800AD
GRAHAM FAMILY ROOTS BEGAN IN WEST AFRICA.

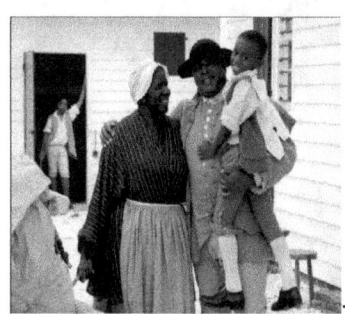-1804 AD
MORAH GRAHAM IS BORN IN NORTH CAROLINA.

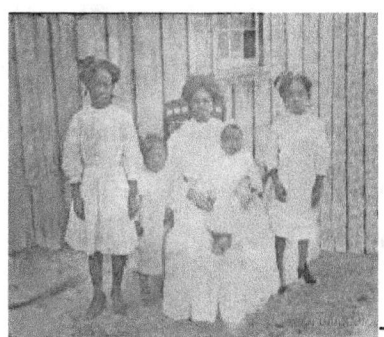-1870 AD
FIRST TIME BLACKS ARE COUNTED IN THE US CENSUS.

ABOUT THE FAMILY CREST

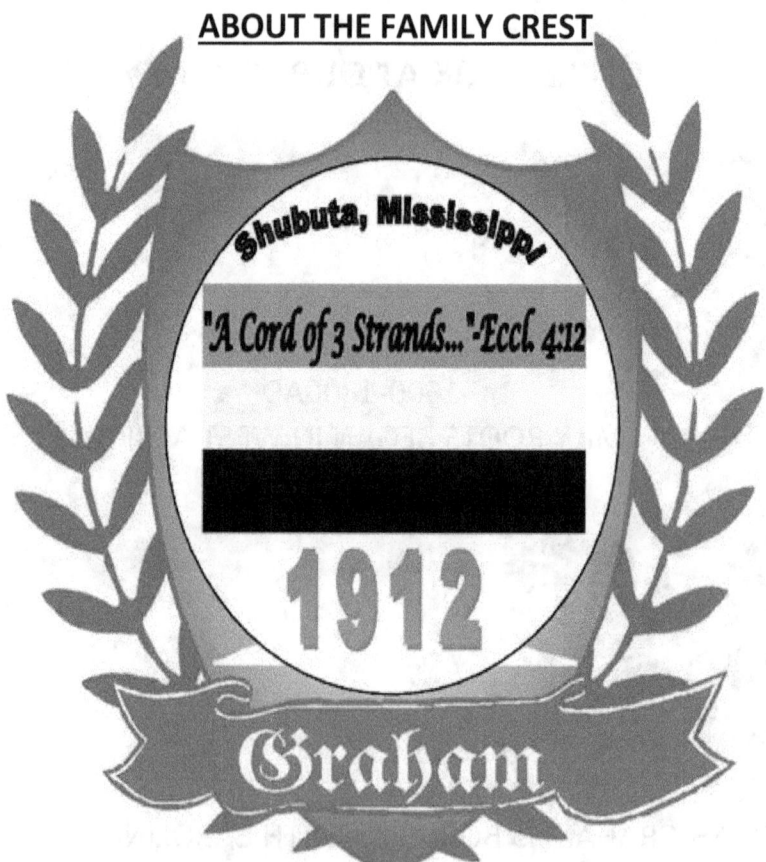

1. SHUBUTA, MISSISSIPPI IS WHERE PINKIE (POPE) GRAHAM WAS BORN.
2. "A CORD OF 3 STRANDS..." SPEAKS OF THE 3 GENERATIONS THAT DIRECTLY FOLLOWS LUCIUS GRAHAM. THE 3 CORDS BEING: MARIVN SR., MARVIN JR. AND MARVIN III
3. THE FLAG IN THE BACKGROUND IS THAT OF SIERRA LEONE.
4. 1912 IS THE YEAR THAT LUCIUS WAS BORN.

"A Cord of 3-Strands not easily broken."
-Ecclesiastes 4:12

"A Cord of 3-Strands not easily broken." ~ Ecclesiastes 4:12

AFRICAN AMERICAN GRAHAM FAMILY
Of Shubuta Mississippi

1912

Lucius Born in 1912
Pinkie (Pope) Born in 1915

Lucius and Pinkie (Pope) Graham

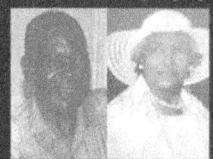

Cord:1

1934

Rev. Marvin L. Graham Sr. Born in 1934

Rev. Marvin with Siblings
Left: Rev. Marvin L. Graham Sr.
Next: Jesse J. Graham
Next: Percy Graham
Right: Edwin Graham

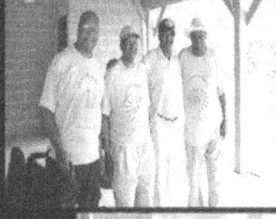

Cord:2

1952

Marvin L. Graham Jr. Born in 1952

Marvin Jr. with Mom and Siblings
Left: Laverene (Graham) McQueen (1954)
Center: Marvin L. Graham Jr. (1952)
Right: James E. Graham Sr. (1953)
Front Center: Lillian (Nelson) Graham Edmunds Born in 1933

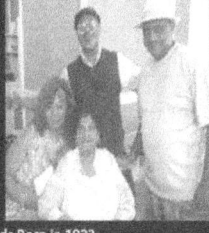

Cord:3

1975

Marvin L. Graham III Born in 1975

Marvin III with 1st Cousins
Left: James E. Graham Jr. (1976)
Center: Laquan McQueen (1975)
Right: Marvin L. Graham III (1976)

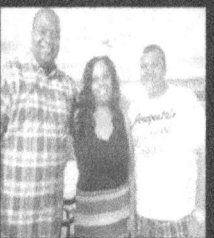

GENERATIONS AFTER THE 1863 EMANCIPATION
Generation 1 MORAH GRAHAM (1804)
Generation 2 PETER GRAHAM (1820) AND MANERON
Generation 3 LONZO "LORINGUS" GRAHAM (1862) AND ELIZA
Generation 4 ALLEN GRAHAM (1888) AND MOLLIE
Generation 5 LUCIUS GRAHAM (1912) AND PINKIE (POPE)
Generation 6 MARVIN L. GRAHAM SR. (1934)
Generation 7 MARVIN L. GRAHAM JR. (1952)
Generation 8 MARVIN L. GRAHAM III (1975)

GRAHAM FAMILY INDEX

Page numbers with (*) by it has a photo of that person.

A

B

C

D

DAVID SR. OF MARVIN GRAHAM SR. - pg 4, *18
DAVID JR. OF DAVID GRAHAM SR. - pg 4
DANTA OF JAMES GRAHAM SR. - pg 4, *22
DONELL OF JANICE GRAHAM- pg 4
DANIELL OF JANICE GRAHAM- pg 4
DAWANA OF GAYLE GRAHAM- pg 4
DIANE GRAHAM WIFE OF MARVIN GRAHAM SR. - pg *22
DEATHA, SISTER OF PINKIE (POPE) GRAHAM- pg *8

E

ELIZA WIFE OF LONZO GRAHAM- pg 2
ED GRAHAM OF LUCIUS GRAHAM- pg 3, *11, *12
ELIZABETH OF MARVIN GRAHAM SR. - pg 4, *18
EDDIE GRAHAM OF ROBERT GRAHAM- pg 4

F

FRED GRAHAM OF ALLEN GRAHAM- pg 3,* 8
FRANK GRAHAM OF ED GRAHAM- pg 4

G

GEORGE OF PETER GRAHAM- pg 1, 2
GAYLE OF MARVIN GRAHAM SR. - pg 4, *16, *18

H

HATTIE MAE OF ALLEN GRAHAM- pg 3
HELEN GRAHAM, WIFE OF ROBERT GRAHAM- pg *16

I

IDA MAE MOM OF GAYLE AND JANICE GRAHAM- pg *16

J

JESSE JAMES OF LUCIUS GRAHAM – pg 3, *12
JAMES GRAHAM SR. OF MARVIN GRAHAM SR.-pg 4, *15
JAMES GRAHAM JR. OF JAMES GRAHAM SR. - pg 4, *21
JANICE GRAHAM OF MARVIN GRAHAM SR. - pg 4, *18
JEVELL GRAHAM OF JAMES GRAHAM SR. - pg 4, *22
JULIUS MCQUEEN OF LAVERENE MCQUEEN - pg 4
JOSEPH MCQUEEN OF LAVEREN MCQUEEN- pg 4
JUAN MCQUEEN OF LAVEREN MCQUEEN- pg 4
JUANEIKA OF GAYLE GRAHAM- pg 4

K

KAMEL GRAHAM OF JAMES GRAHAM SR. - pg 4
KIRSTEN GRAHAM WIFE OF JAMES GRAHAM JR. - pg *22

L

LAVERNE OF MARVIN GRAHAM SR. - pg 4,* 15
LAURA GRAHAM OF ROBERT GRAHAM- pg 4, *16
LATOYA MCQUEEN OF LAVERENE MCQUEEN- pg 4, *29
LILLIAN EDMUNDS, MOM OF MARVIN JR. - pg *15
LEROY NELSON, KIN TO LILLIAN EDMUNDS- *26
LUTHER NELSON, KIN TO LILLIAN EDMUNDS-*26
LONZO GRAHAM OF PETER GRAHAM- pg 1, 2, 3
LUCIUS GRAHAM OF ALLEN GRAHAM- pg 3,* 8
LOREN GRAHAM OF PETER GRAHAM- pg 2
LAJUAN MCQUEEN OF LAVERENE MCQUEEN- pg 4, *21
LAURA TROTTER, KIN TO PINKIE- pg *8

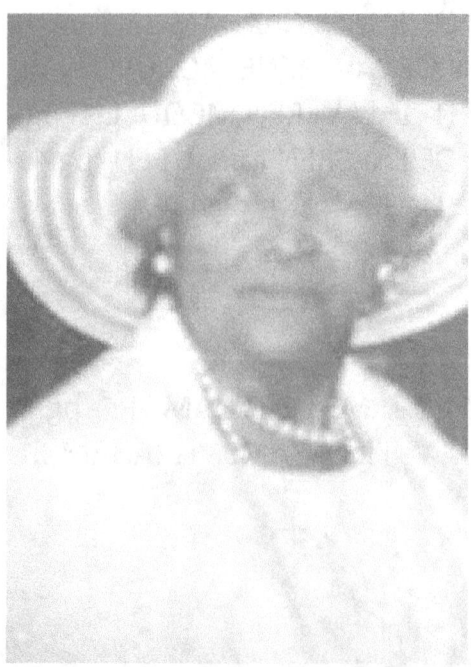

M

MORAH GRAHAM OF WEST AFRICANS- pg 1, 2
MANERON GRAHAM, WIFE OF PETER GRAHAM- pg 1, 2
MARVIN GRAHAM SR. OF LUCIUS GRAHAM- pg 3, *12
MARVIN GRAHAM JR. OF MARVIN GRAHAM SR. - 4, *15
MARVIN GRAHAM III OF MARVIN GRAHAM - pg 4,* 21
MARVINA GRAHAM OF MARVIN GRAHAM SR. - pg 4, *18
MOLLIE GRAHAM, WIFE OF ALLEN GRAHAM- pg 3
MONA GRAHAM OF PETER GRAHAM- pg 1, 2
MARY NANCY (GRAHAM) OF LUCIUS GRAHAM - pg 3
MELANIE GRAHAM OF ED GRAHAM- pg 4
MEARIES WIFE OF JAMES GRAHAM SR. - pg 4, *22
MARZEAN POPE SR., FATHER OF PINKIE GRAHAM- pg 3
MARY HELEN MCFARLAND, KIN OF LILLIAN –pg *26
MARGARET, KIN OF LILLIAN (NELSON) EDMUNDS- pg *26
MAMIE, OF PINKIE (POPE) GRAHAM- pg *8
MARY A. GRAHAM OF LONZO GRAHAM- Pg 3

N

NATHAN GRAHAM OF MARVIN GRAHAM JR. - pg 4
NANCY POPE, MOTHER OF PINKIE GRHAM- pg 3
NELL, SON OF MARY NANCY (GRAHAM) - pg 4

O

OSCAR GRAHAM OF LONZO GRAHAM- pg 3
ORA GRAHAM OF LONZO GRAHAM- pg 3

P

PETER GRAHAM OF MORAH GRAHAM- pg 1, 2, 3
PERCY LEE GRAHAM OF LUCIUS GRAHAM- pg 3, *12
PINKIE (POPE) GRAHAM OF MARZEAN POPE - pg 3, *7

R

R.R. GRAHAM OF PETER GRAHAM- pg 2
ROBERT GRAHAM OF LUCIUS GRAHAM- pg 3
RENEE GRAHAM OF MARVIN GRAHAM SR. - pg 4
RACHEL GRAHAM OF MARVIN GRAHAM SR. - pg 4, *18
REGINALD GRAHAM OF ROBERT GRAHAM- pg 4, *16

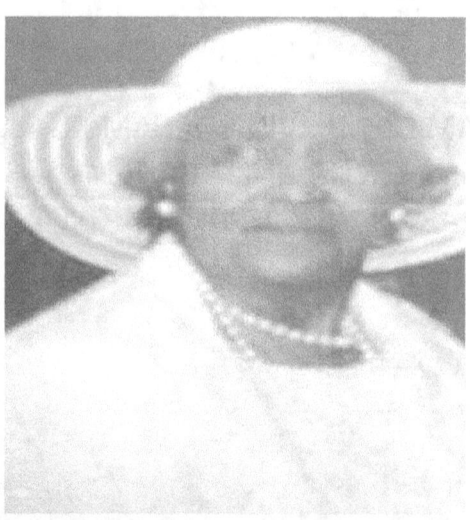

S

SHANNA OF MARY NANCY (GRAHAM) - pg 4
STACEY OF MARY NANCY (GRAHAM) - pg 4, *17
SCOTT OF MARY NANCY (GRAHAM) - pg 4
SEYMOUR, KIN OF LILLIAN (NELSON) EDMUNDS- pg *26
SIMONE GRAHAM, WIFE OF JEVELL GRAHAM- pg *45
SUPT. ELDER JOHN "JACK" JOHNSON- pg *42

T

THELMA GRAHAM OF ALLEN GRAHAM- pg 3
TIFFANY GRAHAM OF ED GRAHAM- pg 4
TIFFANY GRAHAM OF JAMES GRAHAM SR. - pg 4, *22
TASHAY GRAHAM OF JAMES GRAHAM SR. - pg 4, *22
TASHEMIA GRAHAM OF JAMES GRAHAM SR. - pg 4, *22
TASHANA GRAHAM OF GAYLE GRAHAM- pg 4
TRICIA GRAHAM WIFE OF DAVID GRAHAM SR. - pg *18

W

WILLE F. GRAHAM OF ALLEN GRAHAM- pg 3
WILLE OF GAYLE GRAHAM- pg 4
WILLE MAE, SISTER OF PINKIE (POPE) GRAHAM- pg *8

Z

ZELLA, SISTER OF PINKIE (POPE) GRAHAM- pg *8

"Remembering Supt. Elder John "Jack" Johnson."

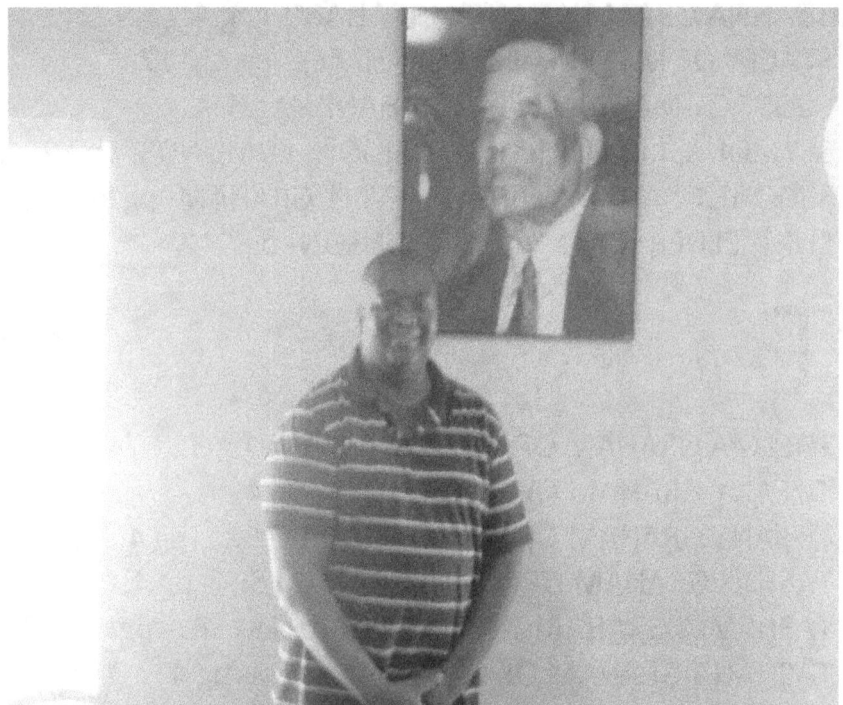

James E. Graham Jr. pictured with Photo of Supt. Elder John "Jack" Johnson who was Founder and Pastor of St. John Church of God In Christ, Albany NY. Supt. Johnson was Pastor of Pinkie (Pope) Graham, Rev. Marvin L. Graham Sr., Deacon James E. Graham Sr., and James E. Graham Jr. Supt. Johnson helped many families come from Mississippi to Albany NY. He was known as "The Black Moses."

Christ Is Preached to an Ethiopian: Act 8:26-40

[26] Now an angel of the Lord spoke to Philip, saying, "Arise and go toward the south along the road which goes down from Jerusalem to Gaza." This is desert. [27] So he arose and went. And behold, a man of Ethiopia, a eunuch of great authority under Candace the queen of the Ethiopians, who had charge of all her treasury, and had come to Jerusalem to worship, [28] was returning. And sitting in his chariot, he was reading Isaiah the prophet. [29] Then the Spirit said to Philip, "Go near and overtake this chariot."

[30] So Philip ran to him, and heard him reading the prophet Isaiah, and said, "Do you understand what you are reading?"

[31] And he said, "How can I, unless someone guides me?" And he asked Philip to come up and sit with him. [32] The place in the Scripture which he read was this:

"He was led as a sheep to the slaughter;
And as a lamb before its shearer *is* silent,
So He opened not His mouth.
[33] In His humiliation His justice was taken away,
And who will declare His generation?
For His life is taken from the earth."

[34] So the eunuch answered Philip and said, "I ask you, of whom does the prophet say this, of himself or of some other man?" [35] Then Philip opened his mouth, and beginning at this Scripture, preached Jesus to him. [36] Now as they went down the road, they came to some water. And the eunuch said, "See, *here is* water. What hinders me from being baptized?"

[37] Then Philip said, "If you believe with all your heart, you may."

And he answered and said, "I believe that Jesus Christ is the Son of God."

[38] So he commanded the chariot to stand still. And both Philip and the eunuch went down into the water, and he baptized him. [39] Now when they came up out of the water, the Spirit of the Lord caught Philip away, so that the eunuch saw him no more; and he went on his way rejoicing. [40] But Philip was found at Azotus. And passing through, he preached in all the cities till he came to Caesarea.

THE GRAHAM FAMILY'S CHRISTIAN LEGECY.

4th Generation
- Rev. Marzean Pope (1898)

5th Generation
- Pinkie (Pope) Graham (1915)

A Church Mother @ St. John COGIC, Albany, NY

6th Generation
- Rev. Marvin L. Graham Sr. (1934)

Pastor@ Grace Temple, Schenectady, NY

7th Generation
- Deacon James E. Graham Sr.
  Rev. Reginald Graham
  Min. David Graham Sr.

8th Generation
- Rev. James E. Graham Jr.

Founder of Christian Corner Fellowship COGIC

THANKS FAMILY FOR ALL YOUR HELP AND SUPPORT!

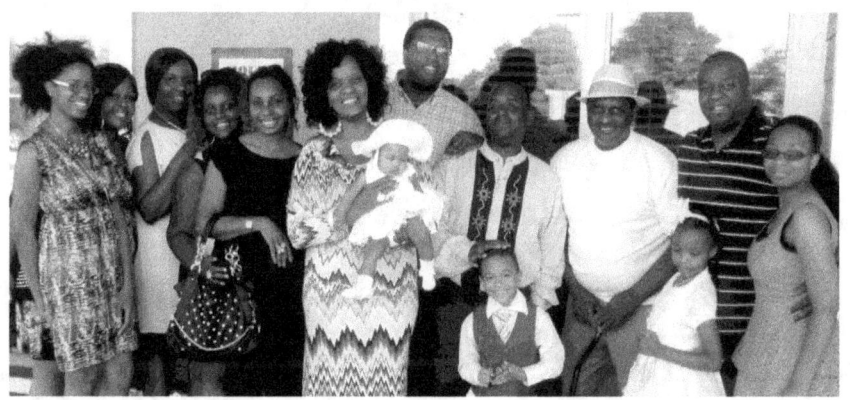

THE JAMES E. GRAHAM SR. "GRHAM CLAN": Simone (Brooks) Graham,
Tameka Graham, Tiffany Graham, Tashay Graham, Kirsten (Speller) Graham,
Mearies (McCarthy) Graham, Holiday Graham, Jevell Graham,
Michael McCarthy, Prince Graham, James E. Graham Sr., Hannah Graham,
James E. Graham Jr. and Hadassah Graham.